Jason and the Argonauts

Author:
John Malam studied ancient history and archaeology at the University of Birmingham, after which he worked as an archaeologist at the Ironbridge Gorge Museum, Shropshire. He is now a writer, editor and reviewer, specialising in books for children. His website is *www.johnmalam.co.uk*

Artist:
David Antram was born in Brighton, England, in 1958. He studied at Eastbourne College of Art and then worked in advertising for fifteen years before becoming a full-time artist. He has illustrated many children's non-fiction books.

Series creator:
David Salariya was born in Dundee, Scotland. He has illustrated a wide range of books and has created and designed many new series for publishers both in the UK and overseas. In 1989, he established The Salariya Book Company. He lives in Brighton with his wife, illustrator Shirley Willis, and their son Jonathan.

Editor:
Michael Ford

Published in Great Britain in 2005 by
Book House, an imprint of
The Salariya Book Company Ltd
25 Marlborough Place, Brighton BN1 1UB

Please visit the Salariya Book Company at:
www.salariya.com
www.book-house.co.uk

ISBN 1 904642 35 7

A catalogue record for this book is available from the British Library.

Printed and bound in Great Britain

Printed on paper from sustainable forests.

Ancient Greek Myths
Jason and the Argonauts

Written by
John Malam

Illustrated by
David Antram

Created and designed by
David Salariya

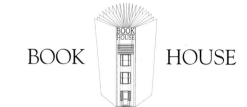

BOOK HOUSE

The world of Ancient Greek mythology

The Ancient Greek civilisation was one of the greatest the world has witnessed. It reached its peak of success in the 400s BC – nearly 2,500 years ago.

We owe much to the Ancient Greeks. They were great scientists, mathematicians, writers and thinkers. They were also brilliant storytellers. Many of the tales they told were in the form of poems, often thousands of lines long. The Greeks wrote poems many kinds of human experience, such as love, friendship, war, revenge and history. The most famous of the poems which have passed down to us are epic tales of courage and warfare, where gods, heroes and monsters struggle against great odds.

At first, all of their stories, lengthy as they were, were handed down from generation to generation by word of mouth. The people who told them were often travelling storytellers who performed in towns throughout the Greek world. They were called 'rhapsodes', which means 'song-stitchers'. As a rhapsode spoke or sang the words of his story, in a loud and clear voice, he stitched its many twists and turns together to make a beginning, a middle, and an end. In time, the stories were written down. What follows is one version of Jason and the Argonauts. It is a tale about a band of heroes whose travels take them to a land far from Greece as they search for a fabulous treasure – a magical, golden fleece.

A map showing the Ancient Greek mainland, surrounding islands and neighbouring lands (below)

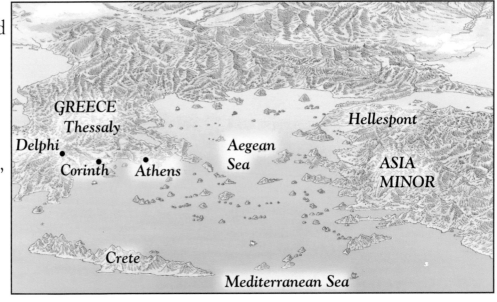

GREECE
Thessaly
Delphi
Corinth
Athens
Aegean Sea
Hellespont
ASIA MINOR
Crete
Mediterranean Sea

If you need help with any of the names, go to the pronunciation guide on page 31.

Meet the storyteller

Greeting citizens. Gather round. I am a the rhapsode – the teller of stories. My tale is about a boy born to be King, whose birthright was cruelly taken from him. His name was Jason, and his future lay across dangerous seas in the faraway land of Colchis. There he would find the fabulous Golden Fleece – the dazzling skin of a flying, talking ram. His mission was to seize the Fleece and return with it. If he was successful, he would be made King. However, once Jason's ship was out of sight, no one thought they would ever see him alive again. Lend me your ears!

I come this day from far away
With a tale to tell that spins a spell,
Which you will hear – if you draw near –
Of times of old and heroes bold.

So gather round and hear my story
Which I will weave from ancient glory,
By joining threads from start to end –
Then you may pass it to a friend.

There was a boy named Jason...

My story begins in a town in Greece called Iolcus. It lay on the coast of the Aegean Sea, in the kingdom of Thessaly. Iolcus had been founded by King Cretheus. He promised that when he died, his son, Aeson, would inherit the throne and become the next king.

Cretheus had another son, Pelias. He was Aeson's younger half-brother. Unknown to Aeson, Pelias wanted to be the next king. When their father died, Pelias seized his chance and declared himself the new ruler of Iolcus. Fearing he might be surrounded by enemies, Pelias consulted an oracle which predicted his future. For stealing the throne of Iolcus, Pelias learned that one day he would be killed by a descendant of the royal family. Cruel Pelias tried to change the future. He murdered the royal family, so there would be no one left to come after him. Last of all, Pelias went after the son of Aeson and Alcimede – a baby boy named Jason.

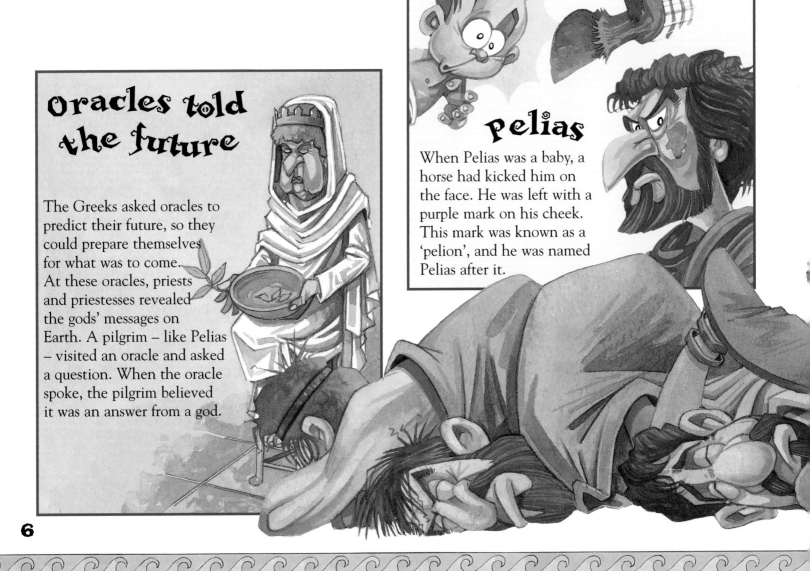

Oracles told the future

The Greeks asked oracles to predict their future, so they could prepare themselves for what was to come. At these oracles, priests and priestesses revealed the gods' messages on Earth. A pilgrim – like Pelias – visited an oracle and asked a question. When the oracle spoke, the pilgrim believed it was an answer from a god.

Pelias

When Pelias was a baby, a horse had kicked him on the face. He was left with a purple mark on his cheek. This mark was known as a 'pelion', and he was named Pelias after it.

7

Raised by a centaur

A mother's duty is to protect her child from harm, and that is what Alcimede did. She pretended her baby was already dead, but really he was only sleeping. When Pelias came to kill Jason, he saw Alcimede and other women standing over the baby's still body. They were crying, beating their chests and pulling their hair. This was how women mourned loved ones who had died. Pelias was fooled. He let Alcimede take Jason from Iolcus, to bury the boy's body outside the town, as was the custom.

Alcimede took Jason to Mount Pelion, the tallest mountain in Thessaly, and left him in the care of Chiron the centaur. Chiron was not like other centaurs. His front legs were like those of a human, not those of a horse. Chiron was wise and kind. He raised Jason, feeding him on meat from hares and teaching him all he knew. He taught him medicine, and this knowledge gave Jason a name by which some know him – 'Jason the Healer'.

Centaurs

In the forests and mountains of northern Greece lived the centaurs. They were wild and uncontrollable flesh-eating monsters, part horse, part human. They liked the taste of alcohol, which sent them into a drunken rage. Centaurs fought mortals with tree stumps and boulders.

Ask the storyteller

Did Chiron tell Jason what Pelias had done?

When he was old enough to understand, Chiron told Jason he was the son of Aeson, and that Pelias had stolen the throne of Iolcus. From then on, Jason was determined to remove Pelias from power and punish him.

Jason sets off to Iolcus

There came a time when Jason knew he must leave the safety of his mountain home. He was young and strong and his heart ruled his head. He had been taught to respect those older and wiser than himself, but there was one man for whom he felt only hatred. That man was Pelias – the man who had no right to be a king. Jason longed for Pelias's downfall.

On the way to Iolcus, Jason met an ugly old woman. She was stranded on the bank of the River Anaurus, unable to cross its fast-flowing water. Passers-by refused to take pity on her. Only Jason stopped to help. As he carried her across the river, he stumbled and lost a sandal. Unknown to Jason, the crone was the goddess Hera in disguise. She too wanted Pelias punished, for he had offended her by not making sacrifices in her name. Hera would protect Jason at all times.

Jason meets Pelias

An oracle warned Pelias to beware of a one-sandalled man. One day, Pelias was sacrificing a lamb to the sea-god Poseidon. In the crowd that watched the ceremony he saw a tall youth wearing only one sandal. Remembering the oracle's words, Pelias asked his name. The youth replied he was Jason, son of Aeson.

I've lost my sandal!

Ask the storyteller

Did Jason know he was talking to Pelias?

At first, Jason did not know the name of the man on the beach. Sensing this, Pelias had time to plan how to rid himself of Jason.

Jason is sent on a mission

Pelias thought he knew the perfect way to get rid of Jason. He asked Jason what he would do if an oracle had given him a prophecy about a dangerous stranger. Of course, Pelias was really thinking of the oracle's warning to himself. It was a trap, which Jason did not see, for he still had no idea that the man was Pelias.

Jason thought for a while, then gave his answer. He told Pelias he would send the stranger to fetch the Golden Fleece from Colchis. But the words Jason spoke were not his! The goddess Hera had put them into his mouth, as part of her plan to punish Pelias.

Only then did Pelias reveal who he was. The young man was furious and said he had come to take back the throne of Iolcus. Crafty Pelias said he could have it – in exchange for the Golden Fleece. It would be a dangerous mission for a mortal and Pelias expected Jason to die.

Fetch me the Golden Fleece!

The Golden Fleece

The Golden Fleece was the shimmering, golden skin of the talking ram Chrysomallus. This winged creature had rescued two children and flown them to Colchis, where it was sacrificed in thanks to the gods. Its fleece was hung from a tree, guarded by a serpent that never slept.

Jason will work for me, and I will protect him!

Oh Hera! What have I said?

Ask the storyteller

Where was Colchis?

Colchis was far away from Greece, at the eastern end of the Black Sea, which the Greeks called the Euxine Sea. It was in a remote area surrounded by mountains.

The Argonauts are assembled

Showing no fear, Jason accepted the challenge that Pelias had put to him. To cross the sea to Colchis, Jason needed a marvellous ship. He asked a craftsman called Argus to build one with timber from the forests of Mount Pelion, Jason's childhood home. The vessel was to be fitted out with oars for a crew of fifty men.

Skilled though he was, Argus could not complete the task alone. The goddess Athena came to his aid. She gave the ship a figurehead cut from an oak tree sacred to the great god Zeus. The figurehead had the power of speech and would guide Jason on his mission.

The ship was named *Argo*, in honour of Argus. It was a good name, for it meant 'swift'. Jason called for a crew and fifty men volunteered to sail with him. They are the heroes of this story, and are known as the Argonauts – the men who sailed in the Argo. At dawn, the *Argo* headed east for Colchis.

Women of Lemnos

The *Argo* stopped first at the island of Lemnos. Only women lived there, as they had killed their menfolk and taken their weapons. Some Argonauts fell in love with the women and wanted to stay with them, until Heracles, one of the Argonauts, called them back to the ship.

Welcome, fellow Argonaut!

Ask the storyteller

Were the omens good for Jason?

One of the Argonauts was Idmon, a soothsayer. He told Jason the voyage would end well, but that he, Idmon, would not live. Despite predicting his own death, Idmon still joined the mission.

Jason kills King Cyzicus

The *Argo* continued her voyage across the blue Aegean Sea, sailed through the Hellespont – the narrow strait that separates Europe from Asia – and entered the Sea of Marmara. She sailed to the city of Cyzicus, where the Argonauts were warmly welcomed. King Cyzicus invited the men to join him at his wedding feast – but a tragedy was about to befall them all.

Anxious not to outstay their welcome, the Argonauts, their bellies full of food and wine, set sail in good spirits, sure they would soon reach Colchis. Barely had they rowed the *Argo* out of sight of Cyzicus when a storm at night blew the ship back to the land. Thinking the Argonauts were pirates, soldiers from Cyzicus attacked them in the darkness. Men who had shared food together as friends fought as enemies. In the confusion Jason drove his spear through King Cyzicus.

Heracles is lost

After the storm, the *Argo* sailed on. Heracles, the strongest Argonaut, challenged the others to a rowing contest. One by one the exhausted men dropped out, until Jason fainted and Heracles broke his oar. The ship came to rest on the banks of a river, and Heracles went in search of a tree from which to make a new oar. Next morning, Jason sailed on without Heracles – this hero took no further part in the quest for the Golden Fleece.

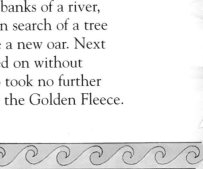

Ask the storyteller

What happened to Heracles?

Heracles, the greatest of all Greek heroes, went on to have his own adventures. He was set a series of tasks, which became known as the Twelve Labours of Heracles. His first Labour was to kill the Nemean Lion, which he did with his bare hands.

The blind man and the Harpies

The *Argo* arrived at Salmydessus. This place was near the Bosporus, the channel that joined the Sea of Marmara to the Black Sea. Here lived Phineus, a king with the gift of second sight – he could see the future. But the gods could take gifts as well as give them. They took Phineus's eyes, plunging him into darkness. From then on, he could see the future, but not the present. This was not all. He was plagued by two Harpies, who stole food from his table and left him forever hungry.

Jason asked Phineus what he must do to win the Golden Fleece. Phineus promised to help on condition that Jason rid him of the Harpies. A feast was laid, and the Argonauts waited for the demons to arrive. When they did, the winged Argonauts Calais and Zetes flew at them with swords and the Harpies fled. Free from the monsters, Phineus could eat in peace. In return, he warned Jason about a danger that lay ahead.

Body-snatching Harpies

The Harpies, whose name means 'snatchers', were the winged women Aello ('Storm') and Ocypete ('Swift Flier'). They swooped down to snatch children and carry them off, never to be seen again.

Yikes! No free meal for us today!

WHAA! Get out of here!

Ask the storyteller

Where did the Harpies go?

Calais and Zetes caught up with the Harpies at the Strophades Islands (the Islands of Return). After agreeing to leave Phineus alone, they flew off to start a new life on the island of Crete.

At the Clashing Rocks

The danger that Phineus told Jason about stood in wait at the approach to the Bosporus sea channel. Here were the Symplegades – two towers of rock that guarded the narrow strait like soldiers on sentry duty. Like sentries, they challenged all who tried to pass between them, moving in until the unfortunate ship was crushed to splinters.

Jason had no choice. If he wanted to sail across the Black Sea and on to Colchis, he had to find a way past the Clashing Rocks. Phineus had told him what to do. Jason released a dove, and as it flew between the rocks the mighty towers shook and crashed together, nipping only a feather from the bird's tail. And just as Phineus had predicted, the rocks then moved back to their waiting positions, giving the *Argo* the chance to slip through the strait unharmed.

Orpheus, the singing poet

As the *Argo* passed safely through the Bosporus, Orpheus sang and played his lyre to calm the other Argonauts. His singing was so sweet it could even tame wild beasts.

20

Phew! That was close!

Ask the storyteller

Do the rocks still crush ships?

Not any more. Their ship-crushing days ended when they failed to trap the *Argo*. From that day to this, they have never moved again and sailors are no longer afraid of them.

21

Jason reaches Colchis

At the far end of the Black Sea, Jason and the Argonauts reached Colchis. All thoughts turned towards taking the Golden Fleece from Aeetes, the ruthless king who owned it. Aeetes promised the Fleece to Jason on condition he completed three tasks: plough a field with fire-breathing bulls; sow the field with teeth from the Dragon of Cadmus; kill the skeleton warriors that grew from the teeth and burst through the soil.

Unknown to Aeetes, the goddess Hera had made Medea, his daughter, fall in love with Jason. It was part of Hera's plan to destroy Pelias. Medea gave Jason a potion that made him invincible for a day – and this was how he completed the tasks set by Aeetes. In return for her help, Jason promised to marry Medea, as long as she returned to Greece with him.

The Dragon of Cadmus

This monster, whose eyes flashed fire and whose body was filled with poison, had been slain by the hero Cadmus. Its teeth were pulled out and shared between him and King Aeetes of Colchis. When sown in the ground armed men came forth.

Ask the storyteller

How did Jason kill the skeleton warriors?

Medea told Jason he must throw a boulder amongst them, causing the warriors to think they were being attacked by each other. As they fought themselves, Jason walked among them and killed them one by one.

Jason takes the Golden Fleece

Did you really think King Aeetes would hand over the Golden Fleece? Aeetes never expected Jason to complete the tasks he'd set him, but neither did he imagine his daughter would work against him! Aeetes wanted the golden treasure to stay in Colchis, guarded by the sleepless serpent whose scaly body coiled itself around the oak tree in which the Fleece hung.

Once again, Medea, whose name means both 'cunning' and 'knowing', helped Jason. At night, she led him to the sacred grove of the Golden Fleece. Even in the darkness its wool sparkled. Medea used her knowledge to cast a spell over the Fleece's fork-tongued guardian, charming it until it was in her power. Then, as she placed magic drops into its eyes, the great snake slumped to the ground and slept. Quickly, Jason took the Fleece and returned to the *Argo* with Medea.

Sleep, serpent, sleep.

Aeetes gives chase

As the new day dawned, King Aeetes discovered he had lost not one but his two most precious treasures in life – the Golden Fleece and his daughter. He sent a fleet of fast ships to chase after the *Argo*, but even he could not imagine what cunning Medea would do next.

He's got the Golden Fleece!

ZZZZZZ

Ask the storyteller

What did Medea do next?

As Medea was under the control of Hera, the goddess made her do a wicked thing. Medea had taken her brother Apsyrtus hostage. She killed him, chopped up his body and threw the pieces into the sea. When her father's ships stopped to collect the pieces, the *Argo* sailed away.

Song of the Sirens

The voyage home was as difficult as the journey to Colchis had been. Blown far off course, the *Argo* sailed to the coast of Italy, until she came to the island of Anthemoessa, whose name means 'flowery'. On this island lived three Sirens – demons of the sea with wings and bodies of birds and heads of women. Their beautiful singing was a sound all sailors feared, as it enchanted men and lured their ships onto the rocks.

This was a fate the *Argo* avoided. Jason commanded Orpheus to sing for the Argonauts and as they listened to their companion's sweet voice they rowed the ship to safety. Only one sailor, Butes, heard the song of the Sirens. He jumped into the water and swam to them.

Ask the storyteller

Did Jason marry Medea?

Yes, he did. They were married on the island of Corfu, where they spent their wedding night in a cave, sleeping on the Golden Fleece.

Washed ashore

From Corfu, a tidal wave swept the
Argo south to the deserts of north
Africa. For nine days the Argonauts
carried their ship overland,
until they reached the
Mediterranean Sea and sailed
for home once more.

> Sing louder,
> Orpheus!

> Let my song fill your ears –
> it will take away your fears.

Talos the giant

> I'm leaking
> to death!

The Argonauts reached the island of
Crete. Here they met Talos, a giant
with a bronze body. He pelted them
with rocks, until Medea cast a spell to
make him pull a stopper from his ankle.
Out poured his liquid metal 'blood'
and his life drained away.

The end of the story

Jason, Medea and the Argonauts finally reached Iolcus. King Pelias never dreamed that Jason would return, convinced that the mission to take the Golden Fleece was an impossible one. While Jason had been away, Pelias had killed Aeson and Alcimede, Jason's parents. Now the time had come for this evil man, stealer of the throne of Iolcus, destroyer of the royal family, to die – but not by the hand of Jason.

For one last time, Medea used her cunning. But, as before, it was the goddess Hera who willed her on, in order to punish Pelias. Medea said she could make new life from old. She killed an old ram and put its pieces into a cooking pot, from which emerged, as if by magic, a young lamb. Pelias wanted to be young again, so he let his three daughters kill him, chop up his body and boil the pieces in the cauldron. Of course, it was all a trick. Pelias was dead.

Are you sure this will work Medea?

Don't you trust me?

28

Jason flees

Jason never became king of Iolcus. He was forced to flee by Acastus, son of Pelias, who became the new king. Jason and Medea went to Corinth, where they settled and had a family.

Happily ever after?

Medea and Jason fell out and she went away. Jason, who was lonely, visited the *Argo* to remember the good times. It was a wreck and one day its figurehead fell and killed him.

Father!

Ask the storyteller

What happened to the Golden Fleece?

Before he settled in Corinth, Jason took the Golden Fleece to the temple of Zeus at Orchomenus, a city in eastern Greece, and that was where he left it.

Glossary

Centaur A mythical creature which was half-man, half-horse.

Crone An ugly old woman.

Epic A long poem about war and the deeds of heroes.

Figurehead The decorative statue attached to the front of a ship.

Harpy A flying creature with a woman's head and the body, wings and claws of a bird, who swooped down and snatched children.

Immortal A being who cannot die, such as a god.

Inherit To receive wealth or a title from someone when they die.

Lyre A stringed musical instrument popular in ancient Greece.

Mortal A being who will die one day, or who can be killed.

Nymph A beautiful young woman related to the gods.

Omen A sign which points to future events.

Oracle A place where you go to hear what will happen in the future.

Pilgrim Someone on a religious journey.

Prophecy A tale of what will happen in the future.

Siren A flying creature with a woman's head and a bird's body, whose beautiful singing lured sailors to their doom on the rocky coast.

Soothsayer A person who uses observations of nature to predict the future.

Temple A place of worship. Most gods had temples built in their honour.

Who's Who

Acastus (a-CASS-tus) Son of Pelias.

Aeetes (a-EE-tees) King of Colchis, owner of the Golden Fleece.

Aello (ELL-o) A Harpy; her name means 'Storm'.

Aeson (EE-son) Father of Jason; half-brother of Pelias.

Alcimede (al-kim-EE-de) Mother of Jason.

Apsyrtus (ap-SUR-tus) Brother of Medea.

Argus (AR-guss) Argonaut; builder of the *Argo*.

Athena (a-THEE-na) Goddess of war.

Butes (BYOO-teez) Argonaut; called by the Sirens' singing.

Calais (KAL-ace) Winged Argonaut; chased the Harpies away.

Chiron (KI-ron) Kindly Centaur who raised the infant Jason.

Chrysomallus (kriss-o-MALL-us) The flying, talking ram with a fleece of gold.

Cretheus (KRET-ee-us) Founder of Iolcus; father of Aeson and Pelias; grandfather of Jason.

Cyzicus (KIZ-ee-cuss) King of Cyzicus; killed by Jason.

Hera (HEE-ra) Wife of Zeus; queen of the gods.

Heracles (HEE-ra-kleez) A Greek hero with great strength.

Idmon (ID-mon) Argonaut; could forecast the future.

Jason (JAY-sun) Commander of the *Argo*; leader of the expedition.

Medea (med-EE-a) Wife of Jason; daughter of King Aeetes.

Ocypete (oss-IP-ee-tee) A Harpy; her name means 'Swift Flier'.

Orpheus (OR-fee-us) Argonaut; a poet and singer.

Pelias (PELL-ee-ass) Half-brother of Aeson; step-uncle to Jason.

Phineus (FIN-ee-us) Blind king; could see the future.

Poseidon (poss-EYE-don) God of the sea.

Zetes (ZEE-teez) Winged Argonaut; chased the Harpies away.

Zeus (ZYOOS) King of the gods.

Index